# Sammy's Walks

## Dog walks in the Forest of Dean

### by Cheryl Mayo and Sammy

© Cheryl R Mayo 2013.

Contains Ordnance Survey data
© Crown copyright and database right [2013]

Designed by David Harris April 2013.

# Introduction

This book is for dog walkers new to the Forest of Dean. You may have just moved here, or just acquired a dog. Or perhaps you are visiting and don't fancy spending half your holiday getting lost.

When we moved here in 2008, I soon realised that although there are thousands of acres of forest in which to walk, it was going to take some time to work out which paths took you back to where you started and which ones didn't and which tracks meant steep climbs and which were more relaxing and would I get back before it got dark. This book aims to help you short cut that process and enjoy your dog walks while you learn the Forest.

The walks described here are tried and tested and mainly keep to forestry tracks and waymarked paths. In describing the walks I have tried to be consistent in terminology: a track is a hard surfaced Forestry Commission track; a trail is wide and generally well surfaced but not normally suitable for vehicles; and a path is either narrow or rough surfaced, suitable only for walkers. All stiles have dog openings.

Before you start out, please read through the points about walking in the Forest of Dean shown overleaf.

As this is mine and Sammy's first dog walks book we would welcome your thoughts on how we could improve it, or ideas you have for further walks. You can contact us at sammyswalks@outlook.com.

In the meantime, Sammy and I hope our book gives you hours of walking pleasure and we look forward to seeing you in the woods from time to time.

Cheryl

Sammy

## Walking in the Forest

- The Dean is a working Forest, and you will come across heavy machinery working amongst the trees and along the tracks. Keep your dog on the lead as you pass and expect the track to be rutted for a while afterwards.
- There are limited facilities: Beechenhurst has a cafe and toilets, and there are toilets at Mallards Pike and (in summer only) at Wenchford.
- When walking on the cycle trail be aware of cyclists and keep your dog under control.
- You will occasionally come across boar: put your dog on the lead and find another path.
- There are dog litter bins at most of the starting points. However, if you are in the middle of the Forest it is quite okay to use a stick to flick the mess off the path into the undergrowth. It is definitely not okay to leave plastic bags of dog mess lying around.
- Finally, the Forest can get very muddy in wet weather even on the main tracks, so always wear suitable footwear.

# Walk start points

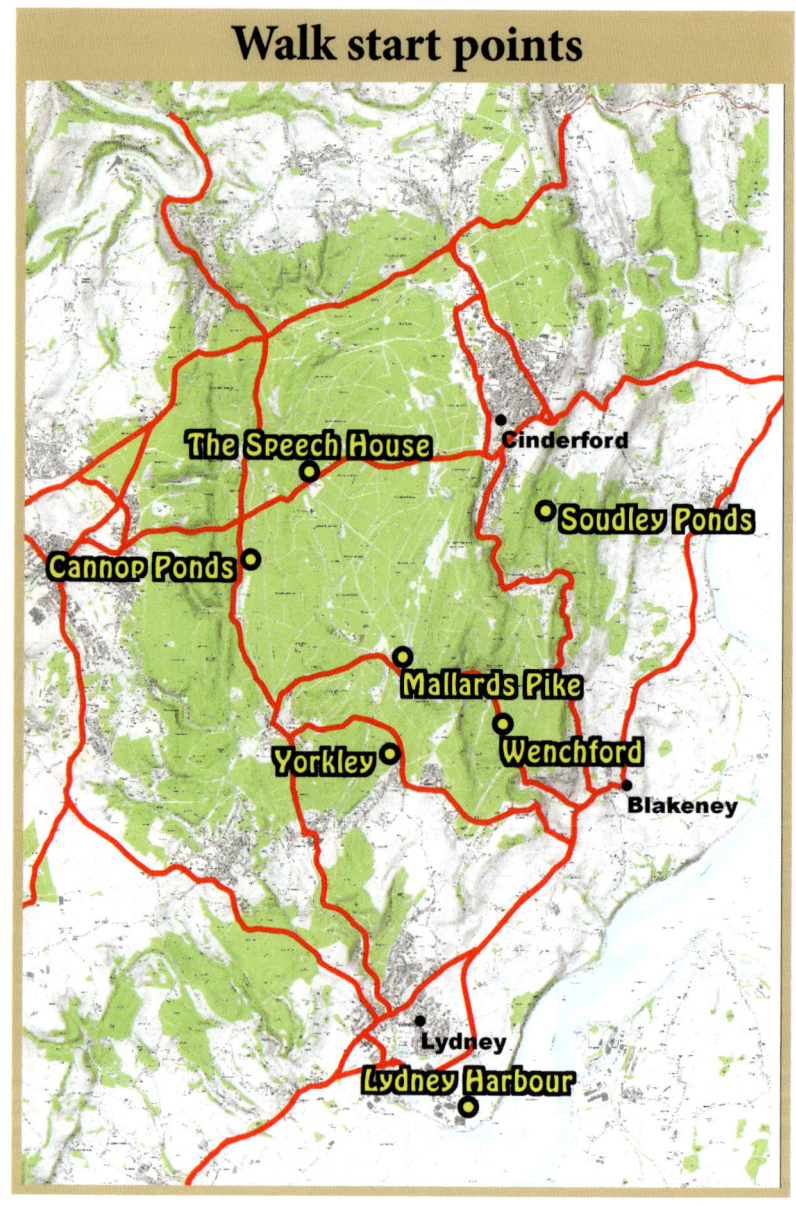

# Summary

| Start point | | Walk | Length Km | Total uphill walking (metres) | Est time | Page |
|---|---|---|---|---|---|---|
| **Wenchford** | | 1 | 2.2 | 56 | 35 min | 10 |
| | | 2 | 3.8 | 92 | 1 hr | 12 |
| | | 3 | 5 | 116 | 1 ¼ hrs | 14 |
| | with option | 3a | 6.8 | 134 | 1 ½ hrs | |
| **Mallards Pike** | | 4 | 4.8 | 65 | 1 hr | 20 |
| | | 5 | 5.4 | 138 | 1 ½ hrs | 22 |
| | with option | 5a | 8.2 | 180 | 2 hrs | |
| **Cannop Ponds** | | 6 | 3.9 | 51 | 1 hr | 27 |
| | | 7 | 4.7 | 150 | 1 ¼ hrs | 28 |
| | | 8 | 5.9 | 127 | 1 ½ hrs | 31 |
| **Speech House: Cyril Hart Arboretum** | | 9 | 3.3 | 46 | 45 mins | 37 |
| | with option | 9a | 4.9 | 80 | 1 hr | |
| **Speech House: Woodlands** | | 10 | 5.3 | 99 | 1 ¼ hrs | 40 |
| | | 11 | 6.7 | 123 | 1 ½ hrs | 42 |
| | with option | 11a | 7.1 | 154 | 1 ¾ hr | |
| **Soudley Ponds** | | 12 | 3.8 | 114 | 1 hr | 47 |
| | with option | 12a | 5.8 | 191 | 1 ½ hrs | |
| **Yorkley** | | 13 | 4.1 | 100 | 1 hr | 50 |
| | with option | 13a | 5.7 | 147 | 1 ½ hrs | |
| **Lydney Harbour** | | 14 | 3.1 | 31 | 40 mins | 54 |

# Walks from Wenchford

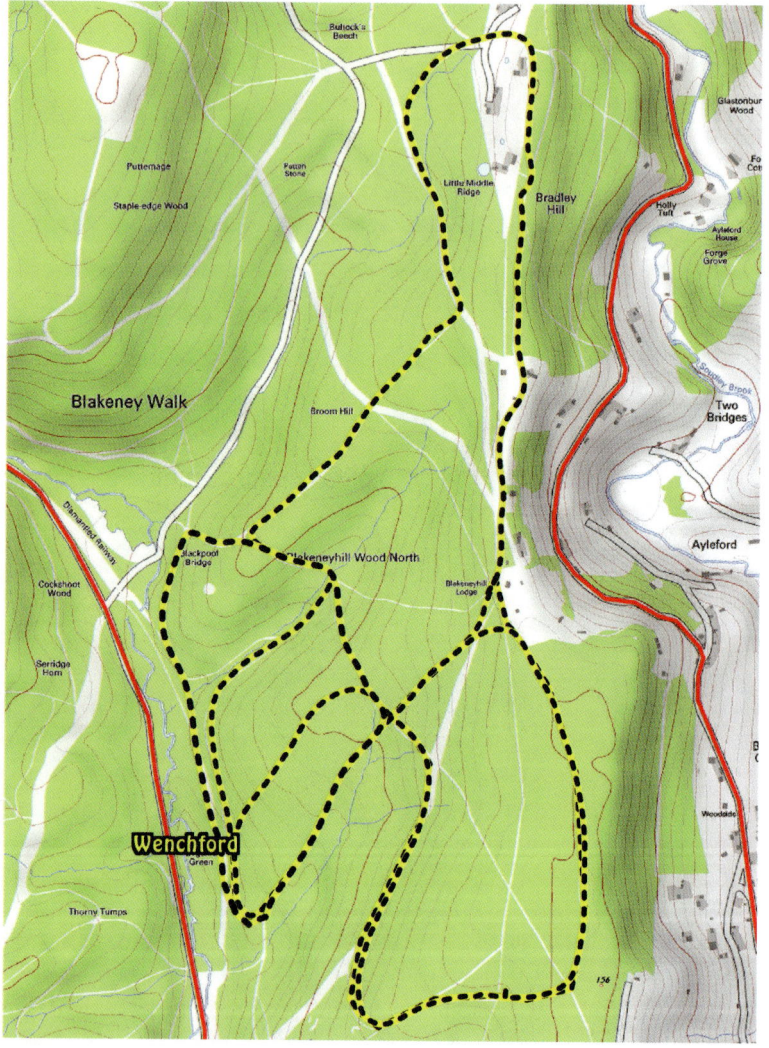

Wenchford is a popular local picnic site. The toilet block is open during the summer months and on some weekends there is also a burger van. Blackpool Brook runs through here and is shallow enough for small children to paddle happily. Pink balloons heralding birthday parties are quite common during the summer. However, for much of the year and during the week it is primarily the preserve of dog walkers.

In addition to the walks described here, you can

» take the green waymarked Blackpool Brook trail, which loops along beside the brook and into the woods nearby, for just under 1 km;
» stroll along the Brook, heading upstream along the picnic area, turning around at some point to retrace your steps;
» take the link path to Mallards Pike, which is marked by white arrows. The return distance is 5 km, mostly along good forestry tracks.

Location: From the A48 at Blakeney take the B4431 Parkend road. Two kilometres along this road you will find the site signposted on the right. The barrier is open and closed daily, with closing times varying depending on the time of year, so take note of the specific time as you drive in. OS Grid ref: SO 654081

**Walk 1 Start point: Wenchford carpark**
*Length 2.2 km, total uphill walking 58 metres, est time 35 mins*

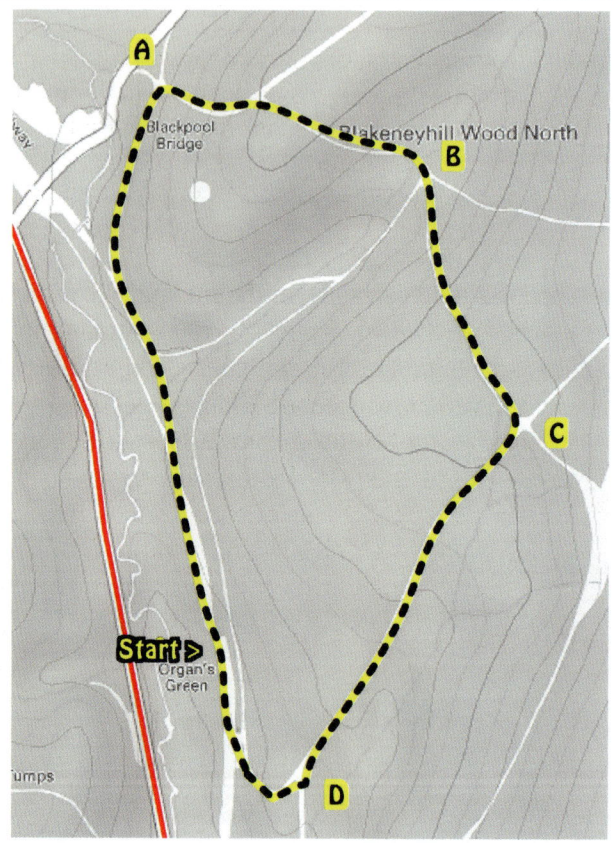

*This undulating walk takes you along pretty paths, crossing streams and rivulets. It follows the Mallards Pike link for a while, and then returns via a forestry track.*

With the toilet block on your right and the picnic area on your left, take the track straight ahead. At the end of the parking area, take the path ahead, past a large stone and go along it to reach a second parking area. A path down to Blackpool Brook goes off to your left, but ignore this and instead follow the sign to Mallards Pike, marked by a white arrow. The path goes down, crosses a small stream and then goes back up to a T-junction. Again follow the Mallards Pike link sign, turning left and walking along a wide path with Blackpool Brook on your left.

Shortly after another link sign, the path forks (A). The link walk continues straight ahead, but instead of following this, take the right hand path up the slope to another fork. Again take the right hand path and, ignoring a narrow path off to your left, continue on this wider path. The path crests the hill and then goes fairly steeply down to the brook (B). Cross the brook and veer right to an intersection of paths. Go straight on and after a bit the path goes quite steeply uphill for a short distance before levelling out. Continue on to a forestry track (C). Turn right and follow the track gently downhill to a point where it bends to the left and descends sharply. Instead of continuing on down, look for a path to the right (D). Take the path and follow it as it bears right, back to the carpark and picnic area.

# Walk 2 Start point: Wenchford carpark
*Length 3.8 km, total uphill walking 92 metres, est time 1 hr*

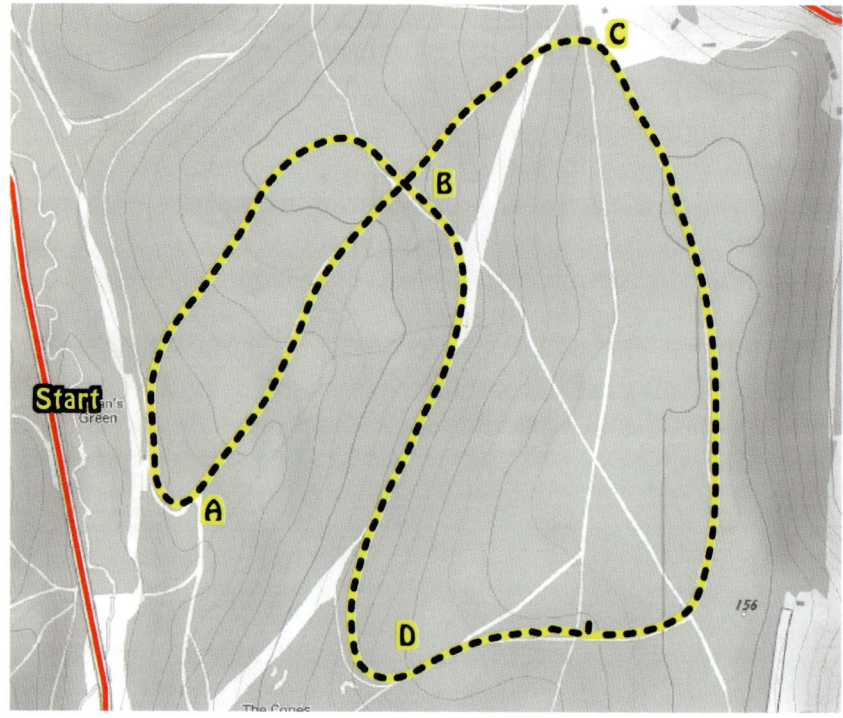

*This walk starts with a gentle but steady climb before coming out to a forestry track which winds its way back down again in a wide loop.*

With the toilet block on your left and your back to the picnic ground, look for the path up into the woods. Go up past a green waymark, and veer right to follow the path up and then around to the left to a forestry track (A). Walk up the track, going steadily uphill, to a junction of track and paths (B).

The main track continues around to the right, but ignore this and go straight ahead, continuing uphill. The path is crossed by a small rivulet which makes it boggy at times, but if you keep to the right you can avoid the worst of it. Continue on towards a large pylon which you can see ahead of you. The path ends at a grassy area, but go straight on with the pylon on your left, over another rather muddy patch, up a short slope and across a grassy area to a forestry track (C). Blakeney Hill Lodge is just to the left and directly ahead of you is a horse paddock which in spring is a mass of daffodils.

Turn right and walk along the track, passing a large enclosure on the left. The track eventually bends around to the right and goes downhill. Keep on the main track passing a number of paths on both sides. Soon after passing one which bears a no riding symbol the track curves to the right. There is also a path going straight ahead, but keep right, passing a fenced off disused quarry on your left, and continue steadily on down, passing under various sets of pylon and telegraph wires. The track then veers to the left and goes more steeply downhill, reaching the junction at point B.

Continue straight ahead onto a path, crossing a small stream. (*You can instead turn left and retrace your steps back to point A and the carpark at this point.*) About 100 metres in, look out on the left for a small path (there are two paths, separated by a mass of brambles, either will do). Take the path and follow it – it can be quite hard to see initially but just keep straight on and it becomes clearer – down through the trees. It becomes steeper towards the end, just before reaching a T-junction with another path. At this point you will see that you are just above the carpark and picnic area. Turn left and take any of the paths back down to your start point.

**Walks 3 and 3a Start point: Wenchford carpark**
3: Length 5 km, total uphill walking 116 metres, est time 1¼ hours
3a: Join Walk 2 at point C, length 6.8km, est time 1 ½ hrs

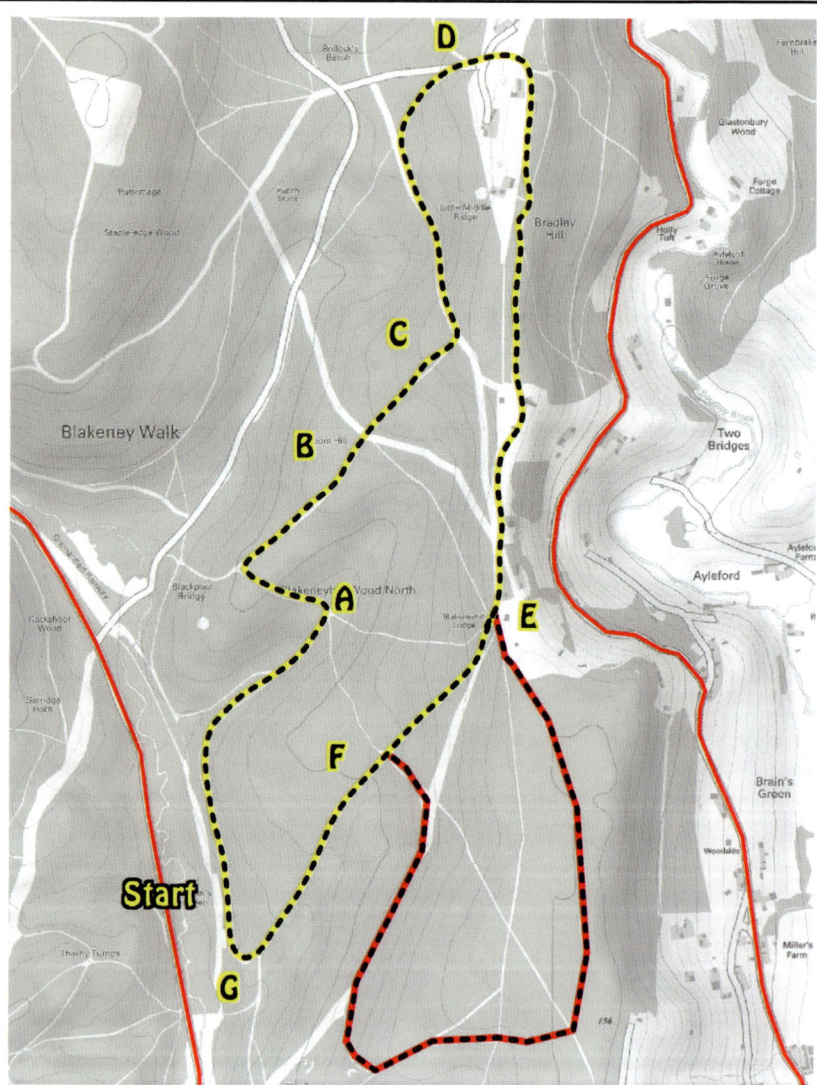

This walk involves some steady uphill work, but in the late spring you are rewarded with a walk through some of the most beautiful bluebell woods in the Forest. You also walk along a ridge line where you catch glimpses between the trees of wide views across the Severn. The longer option of the walk is a gentle downhill stroll on a good forestry track.

With the toilet block on your right and the picnic area on your left, take the track straight ahead to the end of the carpark. Ignore the path straight ahead and look for a narrow path on your right, going up here to a T-junction and a green waymarked post. Turn left and, ignoring the path which goes up to the right, continue on this path with the picnic area and Blackpool Brook below you on the left. Pass another green waymarked post at a path which goes left down to another parking area. Continue on, bending around to the right and with the brook below you on your left. Another path joins from the left. Keep straight on, on what is now a quite stony path, cross a rivulet (dry only in the driest weather) and shortly after this you come to a junction of paths (A).

Turn left down the hill and cross the brook. The path climbs steeply for about 100 metres and then levels out briefly before descending. You soon come to a point where a narrow path goes off to your right with a wider path just beyond it. Take the wider path, turning right, and follow it gently uphill. In late spring these woods are carpeted with bluebells and are quite popular with visitors and locals alike. The path takes you to a dirt road, with a 15 mph sign just to the left (B).

*Bluebells above Wenchford*

*Note: you can shorten the walk by turning right up the road, turning right again where it ends in a T-junction and arriving at point E, Blakeney Hill Lodge.*

Cross the road (take care: vehicles are rare but tend to move quite quickly) and continue uphill along the path directly ahead. The bluebells continue here as well. The path climbs steadily up and ends at a T-junction with a track (C).

Turn left and follow the track. *(You can again shorten the walk here by turning right and continuing on the track to Blakeney Hill Lodge, point E.)* The track goes downhill and then rises again. Continue on and just before reaching a low crest, look out on the right for an unmarked path. Take this at an angle through the trees to come out at a metalled road (D). (If you miss the path, you will end up at the same metalled road; simply turn right to join at point D). Take the road up the hill, past a white house on your right with a red letter box, enjoying the mass of daffodils on the verge throughout the spring. Just past the house you will see a wooden sign for Twilbee.

Keep the sign to your left and walk along the track (the metalled road ends here). You soon come to stables and the house Twilbee, set in charming grounds. Continue on and just at the point where the garden meets the horse paddock you come to a telegraph pole. A few metres past the telegraph pole there is a path off to the left. Take this to join another path. Turn right and keep on until the path ends at a track with houses ahead of you. Turn left, going past Bradley Hill Farmhouse, and continue down. Along this stretch you can catch glimpses between the trees of the countryside across to and beyond the River Severn. Go past a driveway and a gate with a sign Woodside House on your right and keep on, now joining a line of telegraph poles. Go past Hepworth Cottage to a junction, where a dirt road comes in from your right. Bear to the right of the telegraph poles to take the main track and shortly come to Blakeney Hill Lodge (E).

Option 3a: for a longer walk which takes you gently downhill on a forestry track, continue on past Blakeney Hill Lodge, joining Walk 2 at point C and follow the instructions back to Wenchford.

To continue this walk, leave the track just before you reach the Lodge and follow a rough path to the right of the telegraph poles, going through large boulders and on to a pylon. Just as you reach the pylon, there is a path to the right. Take this and walk down (it is quite boggy in places) to arrive at a forestry track which comes in from the left and then bends to go on directly ahead of you (F). Take the track straight ahead, continuing downhill to a point where the track bends to the left and descends sharply. Instead of continuing on down, look for a path to the right (G). Take the path and follow it as it bears right, back to the carpark and picnic area.

# Walks from Mallards Pike

Mallards Pike is a popular Forest beauty spot. The lake was built by the Forestry Commission as a tourist attraction and is named after a Mr Maller, a toll-keeper who lived in a cottage near what is now the entrance to the site. Today visitors can simply sit by the lake and enjoy watching the ducks, or take to the high ropes on the Go-Ape course. Or use it as a very popular dog walk starting point. There are toilets open all year round and a burger van during summer weekends and holidays. Parking is pay and display. However if you live in the Forest it is worth buying a Discovery Pass which gives you free parking at any of the local Forestry Commission sites where there is normally a charge (go to *http://www.forestry.gov.uk/forestry/INFD-7W5Kq6*).

In addition to the walks described here you can

» stroll around the lake edge;
» follow the 6 km circular Adidas Running Trail;
» take the link path to Wenchford, marked by white arrows. The return distance is 5 km.

Location: From the A48 at Blakeney take the B4431 Parkend road. Five kilometres along this road you will find the site signposted on the right. The barrier is open and closed daily, with closing times varying depending on the time of year, so take note of the specific time as you drive in. OS Grid ref: SO 637093

**Walk 4 Start point: Mallards Pike carpark**
*Length 4.8 km, total uphill walking 65 metres, est time 1hr*

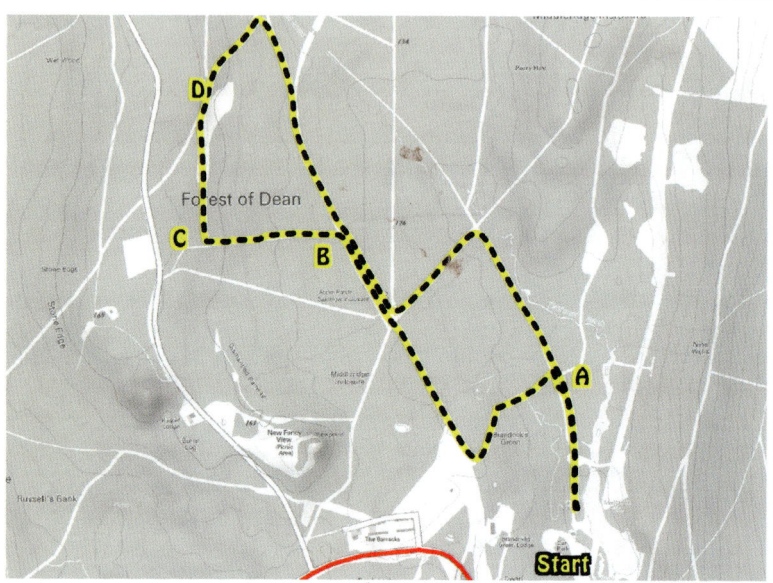

This is what I describe as a "flat walk" insofar as anywhere in the Forest can be described as flat. It is gentle, with varied scenery and using good trails or paths.

Keeping the Go Ape office on your left, walk to the beginning of the Running Trail and continue until the track divides into three (A). Take the first left (marked as the cycle trail) and follow the trail as it bends around to the right and then straight on to a signposted intersection. Turn left and then immediately right, so that you are now on the path parallel with the cycle trail.

Continue along the path, ignoring a grassy track which goes off at an angle on your left, until you come to a path on your left which slopes gently upwards (B). Walk up the hill and, shortly after passing an enclosure on the left, look out for a grassy path off to the right (C). Take this path through pine trees until you come out onto a forestry track. Keep right to arrive at a fork in the track, with a sign to the left saying Trafalgar Avenue (D). Take the right hand track, down a short and steep hill. At the bottom take the track to your right. It soon begins to parallel the cycle trail. Keep on until you are back at the signposted intersection. Turn left, cross over the cycle trail, and at the next junction turn right. You are now back on the running trail, from where you can follow the signs to take you back to Mallards Pike Lake.

# Walks 5 and 5a Start point: Mallards Pike carpark
*5: Length 5.4 km, total uphill walking 138 metres, est time 1½ hrs*
*5a: Length 8.2 km, total uphill walking 180 metres, est time 2 hrs*

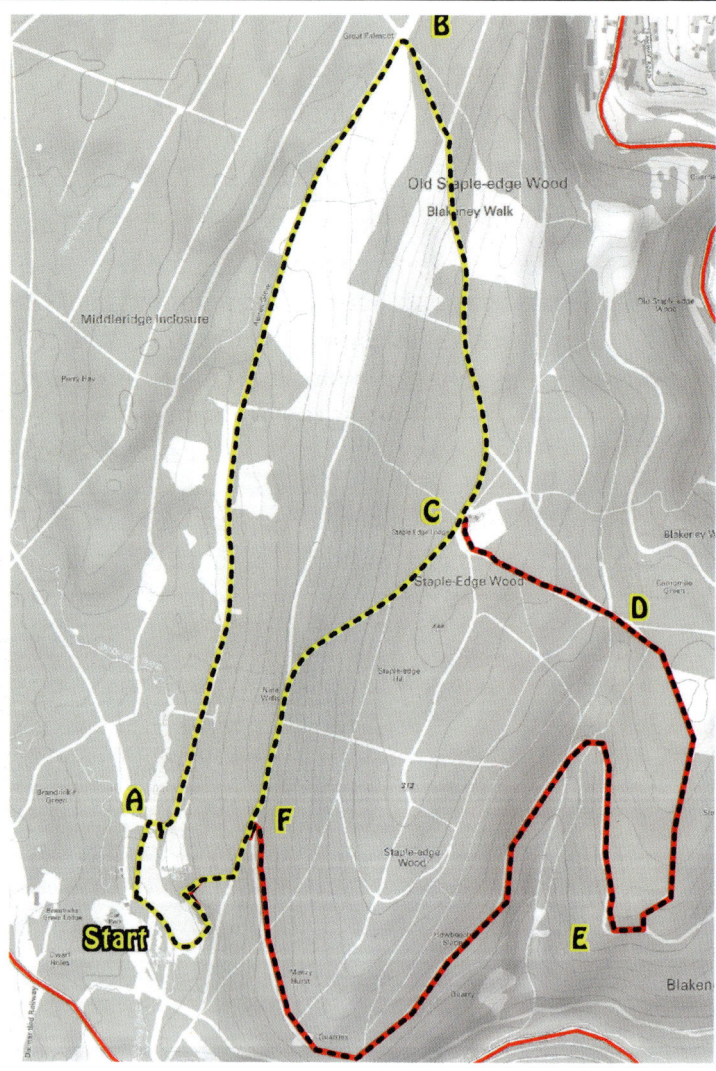

This walk takes you up to the ridge above Mallards Pike, the longish and steady climb being rewarded with far reaching views over the Forest. A steep grassy track brings you down from the ridge and from there it is a short distance back to the start point. The longer option follows good tracks as it winds its way gently downhill back to Mallards Pike.

Walk down to the lake edge and follow the path to your left up to the boat ramp. Turn right to cross over the lake and then turn left, following the line of telegraph poles (A).

Continue along the track for about 2 kms to a T-junction. Turn right and go up the hill to a metal gate and stile (B). *Note: you can instead turn left at the T-junction and then left again to join the Running Trail, from where it is 3 kms back to Mallards Pike.* Cross the stile and then carry on straight over the intersection, continuing uphill, with a post and wire fence on your right.

The track levels out at a point where a considerable amount of clear felling has taken place on either side. The upside has been to reveal some far flung views across the Forest, especially beautiful in the autumn. Just past this clear felled area you come to Staple Edge Bungalows on your left, built in 1809 and still without electricity or mains water (C).

Decision point

To stay on the main walk, pass a stile opposite the Bungalows, with a waymark post behind it. You then come to an opening in the fence from which a path runs downhill (if they have repaired the fence then you will need to cross the stile and turn left for a short distance to reach the path). Follow the path down to a fork, with a waymark post pointing back the way you have just come. Take the right hand path to go quite steeply down to a foresty track, with another waymark post. Turn left and follow the track gently downhill until you come to a wide fork, which is point F on this route. Take the right hand track downhill and follow the main walk instructions from point F below.

Option 5a

For the longer option, pass Staple Edge Bungalows and keep to the main track, going gently downhill. The track levels out and bends to the right just before a T-junction with a post marked M8 on the left (D). Bear right, keeping on downhill and shortly going through a gate with a path to your left. Ignore the path and stay on the main track. At a point where the track goes steeply downhill and bends to the left, turn sharp right (E) and continue on this new track, which winds its way around the hill.

Towards the end of this section, take in the wide views to your left. Just past a large grove of conifers on your left there is a path which intersects the main track. Cross over this and shortly afterwards the track bends to the right, with another track coming in from

*Point F on Walk 5.*

the left (F). Turn left onto this track and then continue with the main walk instructions below.

Main walk continued

From point F, continue on down and just as the track levels out look for a path descending on your right. It's about 100 metres before the white waymarked post ahead of you and brings you out on to the path that goes around Mallards Pike Lake, directly opposite the dog dip. It's easily missed and if you do miss it, simply go on to the white marker and take that path down (always muddy). Turn left and follow the path back to the carpark.

# Walks from Cannop Ponds

Cannop Ponds is a series of manmade lakes set in the steep sided Cannop Valley. It is a haven for birdlife and has a good population of swans and mandarin ducks. There is a picnic area and carparking, but no facilities except for a burger van on occasional summer weekends and holidays. Beechenhurst Lodge, with its cafe and toilets, is only a few minutes drive away however, as is the Cycle Centre.

In addition to the walks described here, you can take the path around the ponds. This can be narrow and rough in many places and one side runs close to the road so be aware of this if your dog has a tendency to run off.

Location: Enter from Speech House Road (B4226), and drive along the metalled road to reach the carpark and picnic area. OS Grid ref: SO610108

**Walk 6 Start point: Cannop Ponds carpark**
*Length 3.9 km, total uphill walking 51 metres, est time 1 hr*

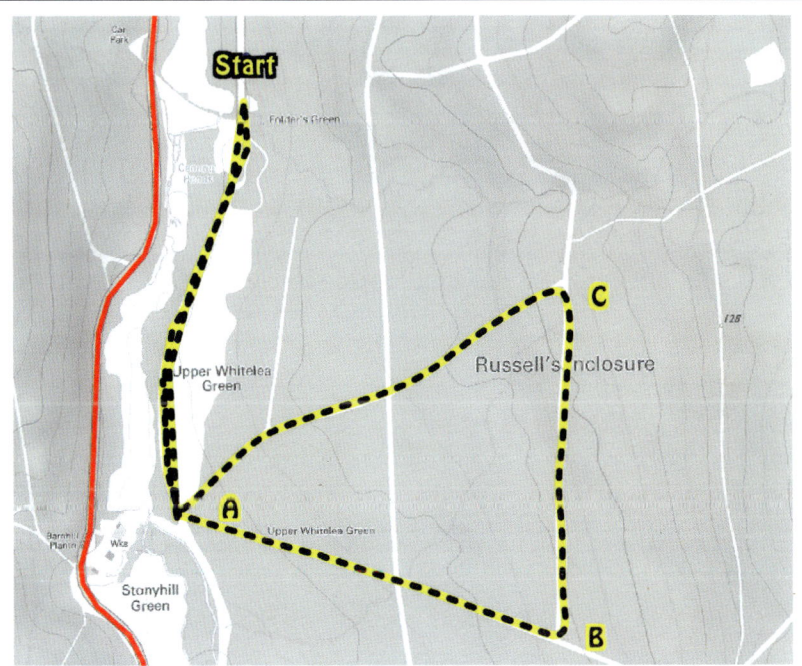

*This is a gentle walk along forestry tracks and part of the cycle trail.*

Facing the ponds, walk left through the picnic area to the family cycle trail (not marked, but you go past a wooden gate). Continue on the cycle trail until you reach a signposted junction and a sign for Cannop Wharf (A). Turn left, following the direction Dilke Bridge and walking gently uphill. Cross an intersection with a path and a stile off to the left, and immediately go through a gate. You shortly come to a track on the left with a marker R1 on the right (B). Turn left and continue to a track on your left leading gently downhill (C). Take this track, with forest to the left and a cleared area to your right. Where the track meets another, cross over on to what is now a path, following the direction indicated on the waymark post by the yellow arrow (also marked Gloucestershire Way and Beechenhurst Trail). Head steadily downhill to a gate. Go through and you will see that you are back at Cannop Wharf (A). Turn right onto the cycle trail to return to the carpark.

## Walk 7 Start point: Cannop Ponds carpark
*Length 4.7 km, total uphill walking 150 metres, est time 1¼ hrs*

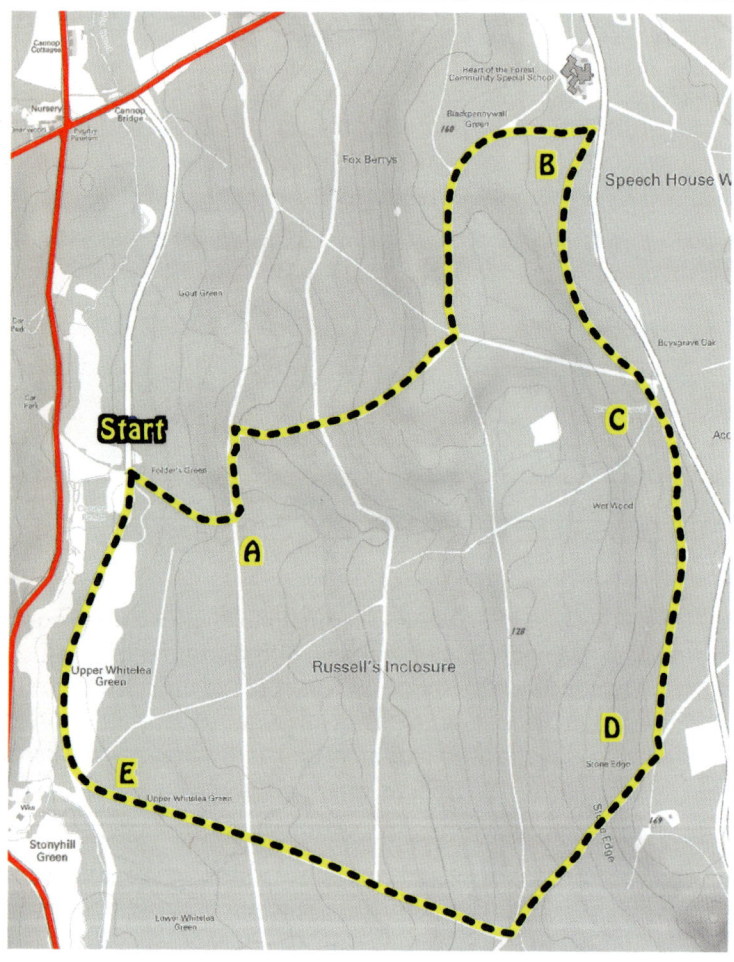

This walk starts out with a short sharp ascent on a rather rough path, then steadily climbs on a forestry track. You then have a level walk along the top of the valley before joining the cycle trail to descend back to the start point. On the way you will see the HMS Victory memorial.

With your back to the ponds, look out for the path at the back of the carpark. (There is currently a red waymark but the Forestry Commission may remove it.) Follow this across two bridges and take the rather rough path (the worst path of the walk) up to a gate which leads onto a forestry track (A).

Turn left and gently ascend to a point where there is a track off to the right, waymarked with a yellow arrow, Gloucestershire Way and Beechenhurst Trail. Follow the direction of the yellow waymark up the hill and continue to climb steadily to an intersection of tracks. Follow the yellow waymark direction straight ahead, still climbing. The track rises steeply for a short distance then starts to level out. Shortly after this the track forks. Take the left hand track, again following the yellow waymark direction. At this point there are mature conifers on your left and younger trees on your right. The track curves to the right and on the bend there is another waymarked post. This time, ignore the yellow waymark and continue on the main track. It curves right and then goes up to a gate and stile leading onto a road, with school buildings to your left (B). Just before reaching the road take the path to the right. Keep on, paralleling the road and going gently downhill. There are great views across the Cannop Valley to your right.

*Spillway at Cannop Wharf*

## Cannop Ponds

You eventually come to a T-junction with a track, with a gate to your left (C). You can go through the gate, turn right and come back inside the fence line across a stile directly ahead of you. Alternatively, look for a narrow path almost opposite the path you have been on and follow this up to a stile. Don't cross, but instead turn right and then almost immediately left to go up to a path with a gate and stile on your left. Turn right along this path, still paralleling the road, and follow it along the line of the hill. At a couple of places you pass some rather large tree stumps which can make ideal seats if you want to rest a while. Towards the end of this section you come across the HMS Victory memorial, commemorating a special oak which stood here for 202 years.

Soon after the memorial, the path meets a track at a T-junction (D). Turn right and right again at the fork, following the main track downhill and passing a plantation of saplings on your left. Pass a sign warning cyclists of a right turn ahead and at the T-junction turn right to join the cycle trail. Continue downhill, past the Three Brothers sign. Follow the trail around to the right and then keep going all the way down, through a gate at one point and shortly after that arriving at a T-junction with a signpost at Cannop Wharf (E). Turn right and follow the cycle trail (direction Cycle Centre) back to the picnic area and carpark.

If you want to take the path along the edge of the Ponds, you can access this via a path to the left of the Cannop Wharf sign. There are various exit points back up to the cycle trail along the way.

**Walk 8 Start point: Cannop Ponds carpark**
*Length 5.9 km, total uphill walking 150 metres, est time 1½ hrs*

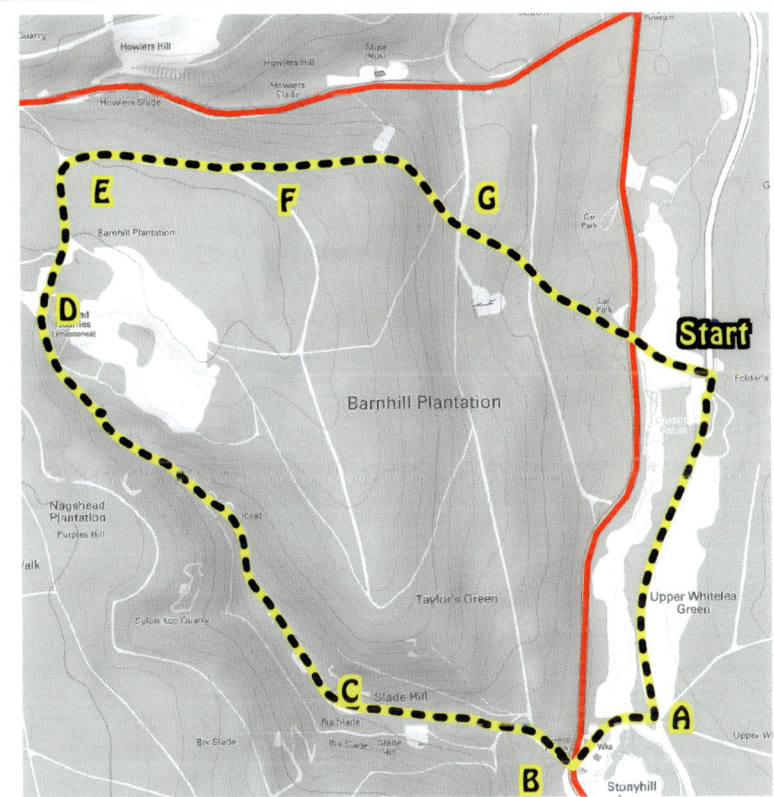

This walk starts out gently enough along the family cycle trail but then crosses the road into the Bixslade Valley to follow the old tramways route up the valley. The climb is well worth it as along the way you catch many glimpses of the Forest's mining heritage, passing quarries – many now defunct, some still in use – and old mine shafts, including a freeminer's holding which is still in operation. You then descend on a pretty waymarked path through the forest back down to Cannop Ponds.

Facing the ponds, walk left through the picnic area to the Family Cycle Trail (not marked, but you go past a wooden gate). Continue on until you reach a signposted junction and a sign for Cannop Wharf (A). Just after the sign take the path to your right which goes past the stone works and on up to the road. Cross the road (be careful, as this is a busy road and visibility either way is not good) and go through a barrier onto a forestry track. Now look out on the left for a path which goes beside a line of telegraph poles (B). Take this path, and you are now on the old tramways route up the valley. You can see many of the stone slabs which are still intact. Cross over a forestry track and continue on the path until you come out onto a track which ends at the gates to a quarry on your right (C).

It is worth making a short detour here, turning left along the track to visit the monument to the United Colliery Disaster of 1902. This is also the site of the still operating freeminer's coal mine (private property).

*Miners Memorial, Bixslade Valley*

Return to the quarry gates and take the path to their left, through the large stones, following the telegraph poles. Continue steadily uphill, still on the old tramways route and still following the line of telegraph poles, passing a group of fenced disused mine shafts on your left and shortly afterwards a disused and overgrown quarry to your right. At the point where the telegraph poles follow a path to the left, ignore this and continue straight on. Not long after, the path levels out and enters an open area with a wire and stone fence directly ahead of you and a large quarry to the right. Take the path to the right of the fence, then the right fork so that you keep the quarry fence immediately on your right. You soon join a wide forestry track coming in from the left (D). There are quarry offices off to your right.

Go straight ahead, under the telegraph wires, and then turn left at the T-junction, along another wide track. Follow this to where it bends to the left and here go through a barrier to take the less well used track to the right (E). Here is a reward for your climb: the road appears a long way below you and across the forest you can see Cinderford in the distance and, closer in, a glimpse of The Speech House in amongst the trees.

*Looking towards New Fancy (top left), with a glimpse of The Speech House*

Follow the track to a waymarked path off to the left (F), following this down into the trees and coming to the top of a fenced quarry. Follow the yellow arrow steeply down, with the fence on your left. At the point where the fence ends, the path bends to the right. Continue on quite steeply downhill, crossing a path and going straight on to reach a forestry track (G). Cross the track to take the yellow waymarked path, continuing downhill to a rather boggy patch. Here the path seems to lose itself, but if you keep going downhill, veering slightly right, you will pick it up again. Continue on to a waymarked post pointing straight ahead. Follow this, still going downhill, crossing a rivulet and keeping on the grassy path until you reach a layby opposite Cannop Ponds. Carefully cross the road, walk along the dam and back to the carpark.

# Walks from Speech House

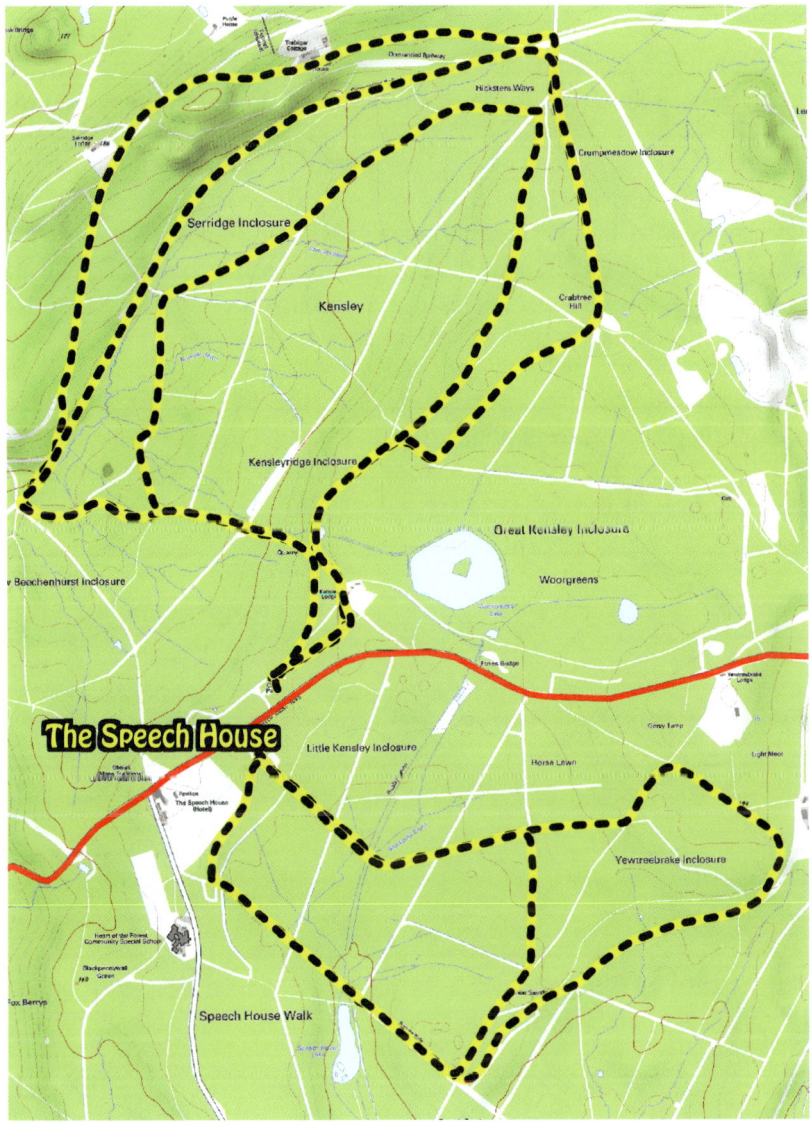

The first of these walks starts at the Cyril Hart Arboretum, located next to Speech House. The Arboretum is named after a local historian and forestry expert and contains some 400 trees. Cyril Hart was also a Verderer of The Forest of Dean and Speech House has been the traditional home of the Verderers' Court for over 300 years. Although now a hotel, the Court still meets there regularly. Speech House is dog-friendly and a post walk visit to the Orangery for tea and cakes or a light lunch is well worthwhile.

In addition to the walk described here you can do the Speech House Walk (5 km), following the green waymarked trail from the Arboretum.

The next two walks start at the The Speech House Woodlands carpark, just across the road from the Arboretum. There is a signed path from this carpark to Beechenhurst Lodge, a short distance away. Beechenhurst Lodge has toilets, a cafe and a gift shop, all open all year round. It is also the start point for the Sculpture Trail (blue waymarks), parts of which are included in the walks described here.

Location: The Arboretum carpark is on the B4226, just 200 metres along from Speech House heading towards Cinderford. OS Grid ref: SO624118. The Speech House Woodlands carpark is a few metres further on, on your left. OS Grid ref: SO624125.

*The path from the Arboretum, January 2013*

**Walks 9 and 9a Start point: Cyril Hart Arboretum carpark**
9: Length 3.3 km, total uphill walking 46 metres, est time 45 mins
9a: Length 4.9 km, total uphill walking 80 metres, est time 1 hr

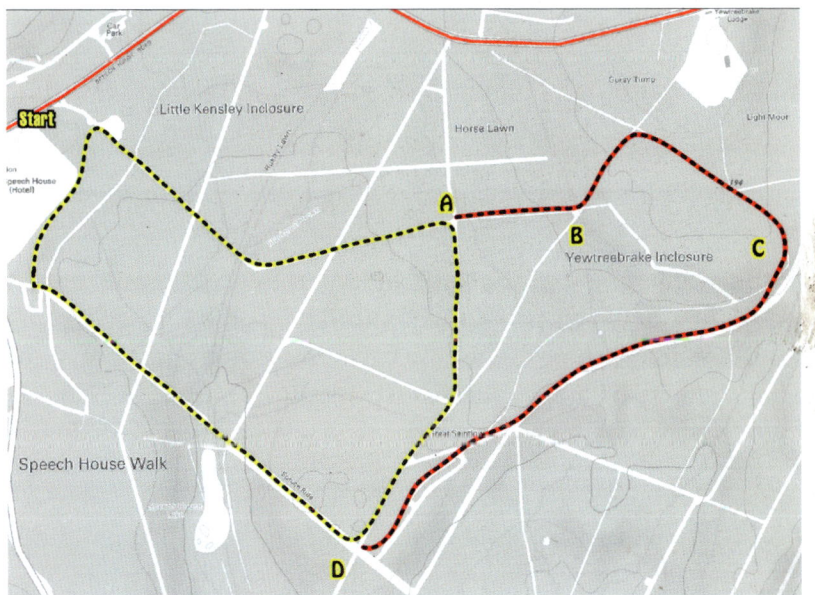

*This walk mostly follows forestry tracks and is very gentle. The last section is along Spruce Ride, an avenue of mature cherry trees which provide a spectacular pink display in the spring. You also take in Speech House Lake, surrounded by mature trees which provide their own spectacular display in the autumn.*

Go into the Arboretum and head straight across to the opposite gate. Go down the path and cross a track with a green waymark. Follow the waymark direction straight ahead. There is a cleared area of forest to your left. The path curves left and then straightens out. At the next intersection ignore the green waymark and cross straight over. The next intersection has a large oak in the middle of it (A).

Decision point

To continue the main walk, turn right and follow the track down to a junction where another track comes in from the left. Continue on, passing a path coming in from the left and then reaching an intersection with a wide track, at the brow of a hill (D). This is Spruce Ride. Turn right and follow the instructions for the main walk from point D back to the carpark.

Option 9a

To take the option, go straight over at the intersection with the oak. Soon afterwards you come to a wide area with two paths coming in from the left and the path you are on curving around to the right (B). Take the first path left which goes gently uphill to an intersection with an enclosure on your left. Turn right and follow the path, with young trees on your right and towering conifers on your left. Pass between two large stones and at the fork go right, downhill. As the path levels out the cycle trail comes in from your left (C), marked by a cycle trail post. Just to the right is a short 'Bikes 'n' Berms' trail.

Continue on the cycle trail, going steadily downhill, passing a path on your right with a double wooden fence and then another one on your left as the trail bends to the right. After a while the

*Speech House Lake*

trail is fenced on either side. Continue on to an intersection with a track, and warning posts for cyclists. Here leave the cycle trail and turn right and then shortly afterwards come to a fork. Take the left hand path, going through an area where the track is divided by a small island of conifers bordered with logs.

The divided track comes together again just as you reach a T-junction with a forestry track. This is Spruce Ride. Turn right, and rejoin the main walk at the intersection (D).

Main walk continued

From D, continue all the way down the long straight avenue to a gate at the end. About halfway, at the bottom of the dip, you pass Speech House Lake on the left.

Go through the gate into a parking area and then look to your right for the gate into the Arboretum. Go through and take any path, meandering through the trees with Speech House Field on your left, and back to the carpark.

**Walk 10 Start point: Speech House Woodlands carpark**
*Length 5.3 km, total uphill walking 99 metres, est time 1¼ hrs*

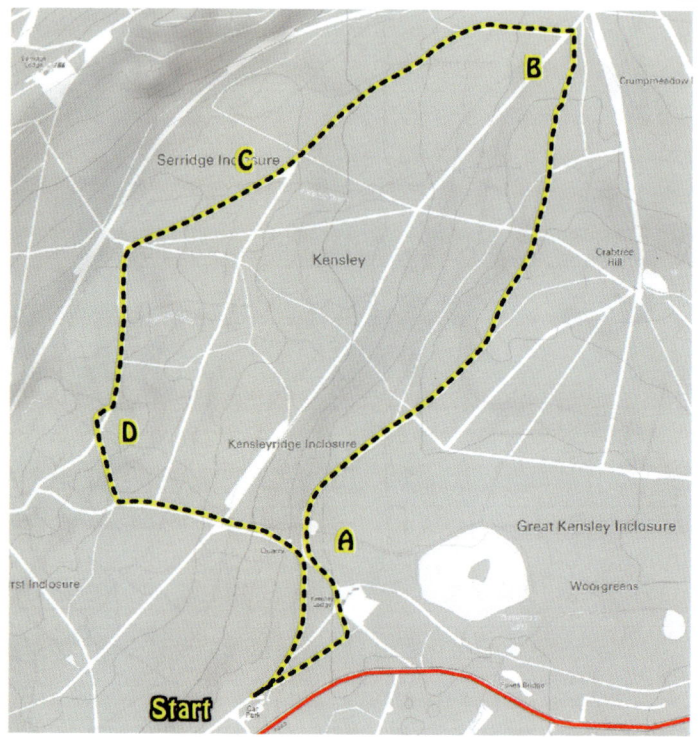

This is an undulating walk taking in part of the Beechenhurst Sculpture Trail. (Visit www.forestofdean-sculpture.org.uk/sculptures for full descriptions of the various sculptures mentioned). Some early parts of the walk, particularly along the Gloucestershire Way, can be very muddy in wet weather but most of it is along good forestry tracks.

With Speech House Road on your right, walk along the path to a fork with a Gloucestershire Way post pointing left. Take the right hand fork, going towards the stained glass "Cathedral" sculpture. Just before the sculpture take the left path then follow the yellow waymark to turn left at the track by a house. Keep left to go downhill to the gates (A). Take the right hand track and follow this past a pond and a yellow waymark on the right. Keep on until the track bends sharply to the right. Leave the track here and follow the Gloucestershire Way marker slightly to the left onto a path. The path rises steadily uphill to another fork where you again follow the Gloucestershire Way marker to the left.

Keep on this path, gradually descending and continuing straight across on the Gloucestershire Way at the next intersection. Descend through the trees, taking care crossing a boggy patch at the bottom of the hill, and continue on the path until you reach a forestry track (B). In amongst the trees to your left is a location marker, C7.

Turn left onto the track which immediately forks. Take the right hand track, with a post and wire fence on the right hand side and a stile a little way along. Continue on this track, descending gradually and passing an enclosure of young trees on your left. At the next junction, ignore the rough trail which crosses the path and take the main right hand track (C). Continue on this track for some time, eventually reaching a blue Sculpture Trail marker. You can make a small detour here into this area which, with its clear brook and hillocks, is a pleasant place to let the dogs have a drink and a splash about.

Back on the main track, pass another blue marker (this one leads right to a bench in the forest), pass a third marker, this time on your right, and then look out on the left for the sculpture "Cone and Vessel". Just past the sculpture, follow yet another blue marker to turn left along an uphill path (D). At the intersection turn left along the track (ignore the blue marker pointing straight ahead) and go past a large fenced in sculpture, "Hill 33", which is (controversially) collapsing in on itself. Keep straight ahead and cross over the next intersection. To your right is another location marker, C2, and on the left another blue marker. Keep on, up the quite steep hill, passing the "Echo" sculpture on your left and continuing up to the gates at A.

Just before the gates there is a single gate and path off to the right, marked the Gloucestershire Way. Take this path back to the carpark. (If it appears very muddy, then retrace your steps, following the blue markers or the yellow waymarks back to the carpark.)

**Walks 11 and 11a Start point: Speech House Woodlands carpark**
*11: Length 6.1 km, total uphill walking 123 metres, est time 1½ hrs*
*11a: Length 7.1 km, total uphill walking 154 metres, est time 1¾ hrs*

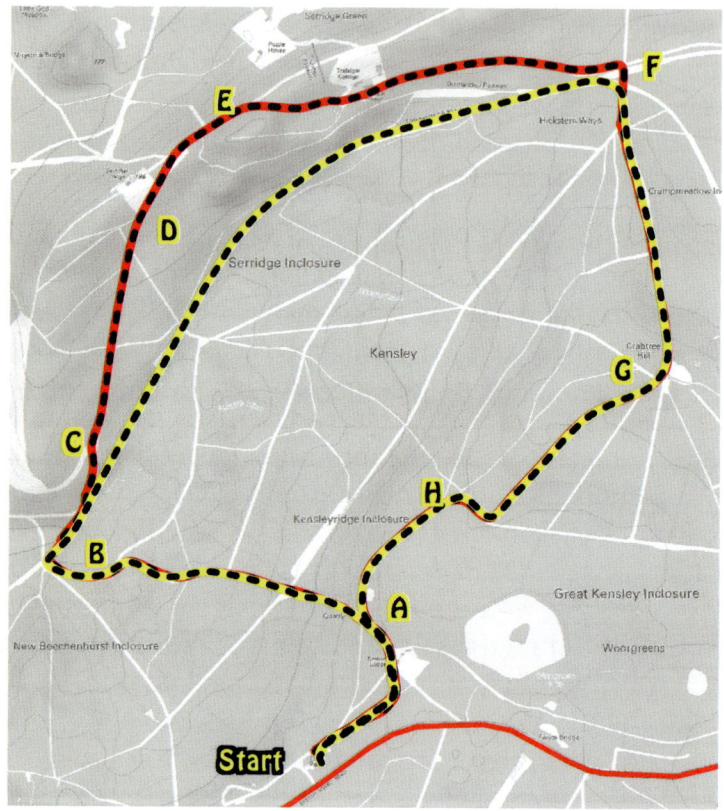

Much of this walk is along forestry tracks or the cycle trail. It also takes in some of the Beechenhurst Sculpture Trail. (Visit www.forestofdean-sculpture.org.uk/sculptures for full descriptions of the sculptures mentioned.) The more vigorous option takes you up to a ridge line via a steady uphill climb, and then brings you back down along the Wysis Way, following pretty woodland paths.

With Speech House Road on your right, walk along the path to a fork with a Gloucestershire Way post pointing left. Take the right hand fork, going towards the stained glass "Cathedral" sculpture. Just before the sculpture take the left path then follow the yellow waymark to turn left at the track by a house. Keep left to go downhill to the gates (A). Continue straight on downhill, shortly passing the "Echo" sculpture on your right. Go straight across the intersection (marked C2). Pass a track going off to your right and immediately pass the fenced in sculpture "Hill 33" which is (controversially) collapsing in on itself.

Continue down, crossing a path with a blue waymark. The track bends a little to the right and then sweeps left, with another track coming in from the right. Keep left, crossing a stream and continuing on to a junction of tracks marked C3. Go downhill and through the white gate (B). On the other side is a sign saying "White Gates" and a signposted cycle trail marker.

Turn immediately right and follow the trail, passing the Iron Road sculpture and then coming to a wooden barrier.

Decision point

To stay on the main walk, keep straight on at this point and follow the trail all the way to Drybrook Road Station. The trail follows the path of a disused railway track with broadleaves the dominant trees on either side. Along the way you will pass beneath an

old ivy-covered railway bridge. Shortly after the bridge you pass a short roughly circular path to the left signed "Reversing the grade". Eventually you come out to a metalled track and the sign for Drybrook Road Station (F). Leave the cycle trail here and turn right on to the metalled track. Now follow the main walk instructions from point F below.

Option 11a

At the wooden barrier, leave the cycle trail and turn left, going uphill on a broad track signposted Branch to Lydbrook. The track soon swings to the left, but as it does so, look out for a path on your right (C). Take this path and at the next fork go left.

This is the beginning of a steady ascent through the trees. Continue on up until you reach a plantation of saplings to your right. You then come to a house on your left with a drystone wall marking the boundary (D). There is a sign here, on the right, indicating that this is part of the Wysis Way. Keeping the house on your left, continue on to a barrier, go through it and then turn right to go through another barrier, with the house now behind you. Walk on, looking out on the right for a stile, which has a yellow waymark and a Wysis Way sign (E). Cross the stile and take the path down through the mature beech and oak trees to another stile. Cross the stile and walk over to the track ahead of you. Turn right and follow the track past two houses on your left, after which the track becomes a path. There are some old stone buildings on the left. Continue on this woodland path, eventually coming out to a metalled track.

The Wysis Way goes straight ahead, but turn right and cross the cycle trail, signed Drybrook Road Station (F). You are now back on the main walk.

Main walk continued

Continue down through a barrier. Keep left where the track forks at some boulders and continue on the metalled track. It eventually starts to climb quite steeply but after a short distance you reach the top and a junction of paths and tracks (G). Leave the road here, bearing right and taking the first path left. Ignore the path with the yellow waymark sign pointing directly ahead. Walk through this large cleared area, through gorse bushes here and there, until you come to a forestry track. Turn right and shortly afterwards the track curves left, going slightly downhill. The track – and the path to your right – is now part of the Gloucestershire Way (unmarked here)(H). Follow the track to the left, pass a yellow waymark on your right and then a pond and another yellow waymark on your left. Soon after the pond, follow the track around to the left at a T-junction, to arrive back at point A.

Just before you reach point A, there is a single gate and path off to the right, marked the Gloucestershire Way. Take this path back to the carpark. (If it appears very muddy, retrace your steps, following the blue markers or the yellow waymarks back to the carpark.)

# A Walk from Soudley Ponds

Soudley Ponds is a series of man-made ponds set in a small steep sided valley and surrounded by huge Douglas fir trees. The path around the ponds provides a beautiful and easy stroll for local people, visitors and dog walkers. There are no facilities, but the Dean Heritage Museum which is located on the opposite side of the road at the far end of the Ponds, has a cafe and "dog parking", complete with water bowl.

Location: The carpark is located on the minor Soudley to Littledean Road, about a kilometre along on the right hand side (there is no sign but the entrance is obvious). OS Grid ref: SO668114

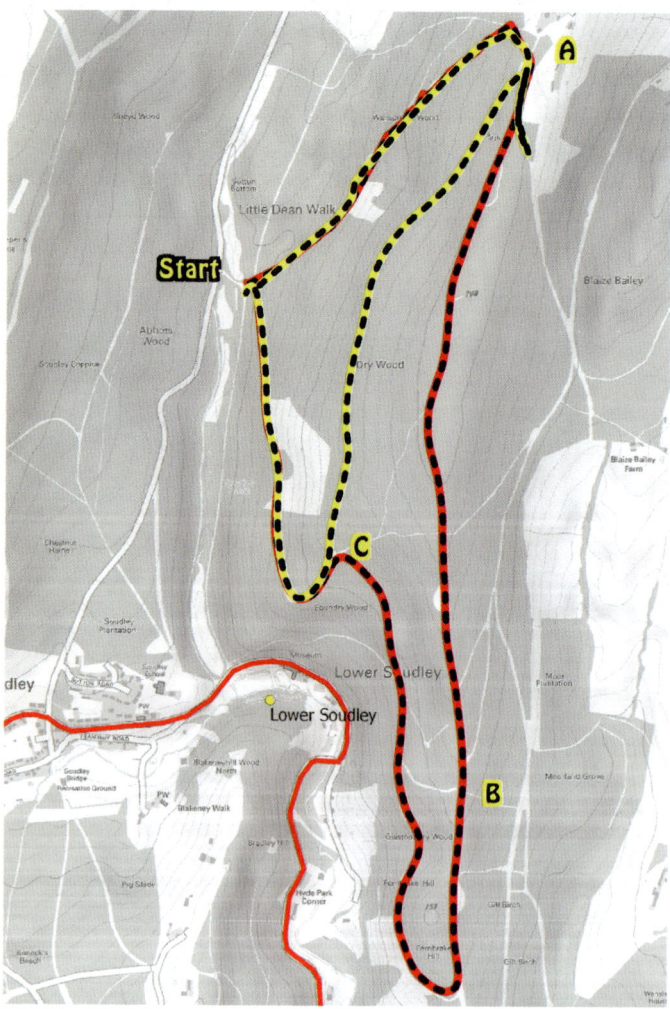

**Walks 12 and 12a Start point: carpark on the Soudley-Littledean Rd**
*12: Length 3.8 km, total uphill walking 114 metres, est time 1 hr*
*12a: Length 5.8 km, total uphill walking 191 metres, est time 1½ hrs*

*This walk starts out with a fairly stiff climb, rewarded by the views across the Severn from the Blaize Bailey viewpoint. After that, it's all downhill, along a path which follows the contour of the hill – with some great forest views along the way–and then meets up with the longer option to descend to the carpark. The option undulates but gradually takes you back down via a large loop. There are lovely views across the valley in the latter part of the walk.*

Walk through the barrier at the back of the carpark to a meeting of three forestry tracks. Take the middle track and climb steadily up to the top. As the track bends to the right, with a house on the left, you will see a path going off to the right. Pass this and continue up for a little way until you see a fork in the tracks and a yellow waymark pointing left (A). Follow the waymark and you immediately come to the Blaize Bailey viewpoint, giving you panaromic views across the Severn and up to the Cotswolds. Retrace your steps back to the fork.

*The view from Blaize Bailey, Soudley Ponds*

Decision point

To continue the main walk, go back down to the path opposite the house. Turn left to follow the path gently downhill. You eventually come out at a forestry track (C). Opposite you is a grove of beech trees which are splendid in the autumn. Turn right on this track with the beech trees on your left, and wind your way downhill until you are back at the carpark.

Option 12a

For the option, take the right hand track (as you face towards the lookout) at the fork. From this point you simply continue on the main track, passing a number of paths on both sides. At one point another track comes in from the left (B) and after a while the track then sweeps downhill around to the right, giving you lovely views over the valley with some houses down below. There is a brief uphill shortly after this, going up to a grove of beech trees on the left which are splendid in the autumn. Here the track joins the path (on your right) from the main walk (C). Continue on the main track which bends around to the right and then winds its way downhill back to the carpark.

# A walk from Yorkley

There are numerous laybys beside most Forest roads where locals park to start their dog walks. I have chosen this one just outside the village of Yorkley as a good example of a "local walk".

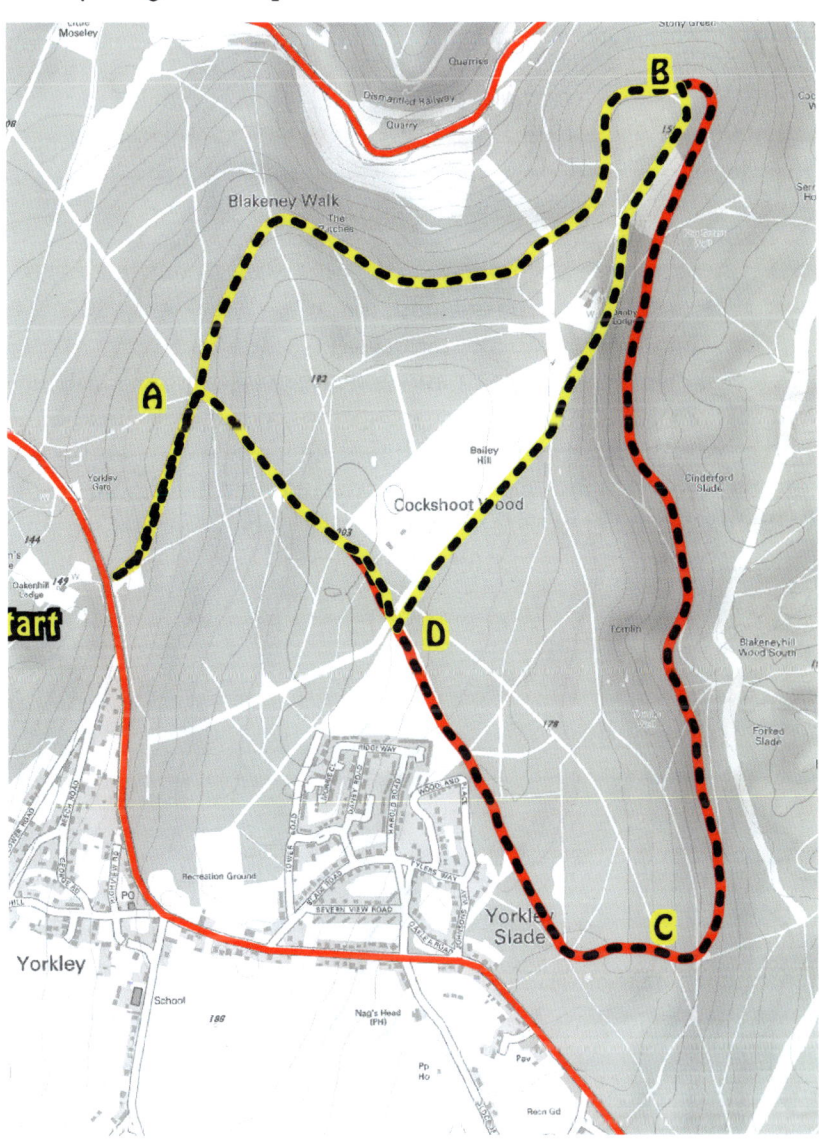

**Walks 13 and 13a Start point:** Layby outside Yorkley, on the right just past the delimited speed signs heading towards Parkend.
13: Length 3.7 km, total uphill walking 87 metres, est time 1 hr
13a: Length 5.7 km, total uphill walking 147 metres, est time 1½ hrs

This walk starts out on a forestry track, and then takes you further up into the woods to go past Danby Lodge, formerly a forest manager's lodge and now a private home. Enjoy lovely views across the valley before descending via a grassy track back to your start point. The longer option misses Danby Lodge, but I have noted where you can make a short detour to see it if you wish.

Go through the barrier and along the track, with beech and oak to your right and conifers to the left. Pass under the telegraph wires and continue straight ahead, across an intersection with a path (A). Cross over the next path and continue on, passing a stile on your left as you follow the track around to the right. At this point the valley falls away quite steeply to your left. Go past an uphill path on your right and descend steadily. Pass another uphill track to the right and shortly afterwards pass under more telegraph wires. Follow the track until it climbs uphill and sweeps around to the right. As you reach the crest you will see that the track descends and curves right.

Decision point

To stay on the main walk, look out here for a wide path which goes up on your right (B).

Follow the path up and around to the right. A little way along there is a bench set at a point to take advantage of a spectacular view through the trees. The path climbs steadily to a fork. Keep left, passing Danby Lodge above you on your right and admiring the views to your left. At the next fork, keep right and pass through a gate next to a barrier. Here you can get a good view of the Lodge. Opposite you is a horse paddock. Take the forestry track which goes off to the left (NOT the path to the left of the forestry track) and follow that, keeping the paddocks on your right.

Pass a track on your right which leads to some houses and shortly afterwards you come to an intersection with a path (D). The lines of telegraph poles also intersect here. Turn right and follow the instructions below for the main walk from point D.

Option 13a

For the option, continue downhill on the main track, continuing to bear right. The track winds its way around the contour of the hill with a number of rutted and steep logging tracks off to the right and left. Ignore all these and keep to the main track, which starts to ascend, at first gently and then more steeply. As the track levels out you come to a five way junction (C). Ignore the track immediately to your right, which heads back in the direction you have come from, and take the right hand track which goes up the hill. It's quite steep but soon levels out.

Cross an intersection with a path with a no riding symbol, continue on, ignoring another path to the right and noting the old quarry to your left. Go past a path to the left to reach a line of telegraph poles and a path off to the right with another no rid-

ing symbol. Take this path, following the line of telegraph poles through a grassy area with the outskirts of the village of Yorkley to your left. Keep following the telegraph poles to an intersection with a dirt road, with a couple of houses on the other side of the road and off to the right (D).

Cross the road and then follow the main walk instructions below. *Note: if you wish to see Danby Lodge, turn right along the dirt road and the Lodge is a short distance along, past the horse paddocks.*

Main walk continued

Go downhill on the path below the telegraph poles. Cross an intersection of paths, and continue on to the track at point A. Turn left and retrace your steps back to the layby.

# A walk from Lydney Harbour

Lydney Harbour is a scheduled ancient monument. The harbour was built to transport iron and later coal from the Forest and the current canal and basin complex was built by the Severn and Wye Railway and Canal Company at the beginning of the 19th century. At its peak, around 300,000 tons of coal was being exported annually in over 2,000 vessels. The final export of coal from the harbour was in 1960. Today it is home to the Lydney Yacht Club and a popular spot for dog walkers. There are a couple of picnic tables and a large grassed area but no facilities.

In addition to the walk described here you can take the path which runs beside the canal to head back towards Lydney Station. Turn right at the signpost opposite the picnic tables. Note that this is not a circular walk and you need to turn around at the end of the path and retrace your steps.

Location: From the A48 Lydney bypass, follow the signs for the train station. Continue past the station and keep going to the end of the road. Park on the side of the road in front of the old harbour buildings. OS Grid ref: SO 6498013

*The River Severn at low tide*

**Walk 14 Start point: Parking at the end of the road to Lydney Harbour, in front of the old harbour buildings.**
*Length 3.1 km, total uphill walking 31 metres, est time 40 min*

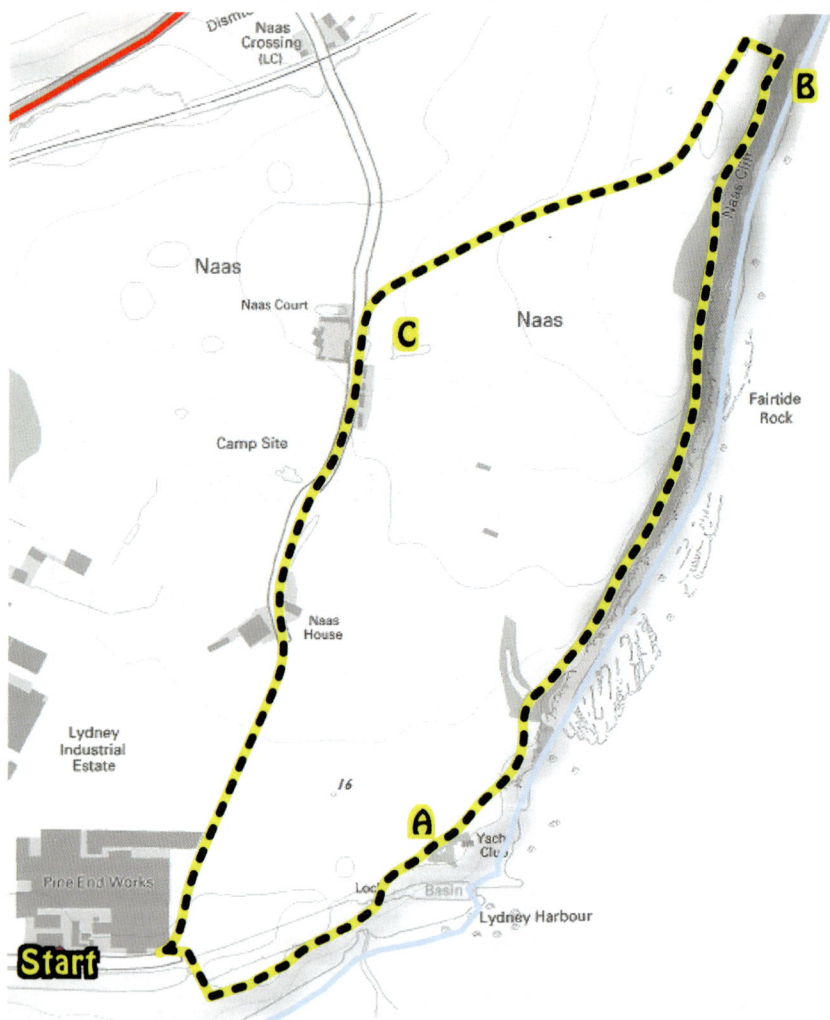

This is a varied and pretty walk with great views up and down the River Severn and across country towards the Forest of Dean. Please note that the walk takes you through a wooded area along the cliffs above the Severn. The path itself is not dangerous but it is recommended that young dogs, or dogs likely to chase squirrels and rabbits should be kept on the lead for at least parts of the walk. Similarly, if walking with children, ensure that they keep to the path.

With your back to the old harbour buildings you will see a bridge over the canal with a metal gate at the far end. Go through the gate and straight on, coming out to a wide grassy area with picnic tables which overlooks the Severn. There are wonderful views down the river to the Severn Bridge. If you are lucky enough to have timed your walk right, you might witness the incoming or outgoing tides which rush through here with some turbulence.

Turn left, taking either of the two paths down to the lock gates which cross the canal. Cross any one of these and then look along the bank opposite for the wooden steps near the two old stone buildings (the former morgue and store) (A). Go up the steps to come out at the edge of a cultivated field. Turn right and take the path along the top of the bank with the Yacht Club below you. The path bends around to the left and then you come across an opening off to your right which takes you in amongst the trees. Follow this path down the dip and up again, keeping straight on at the waymarked fork. You are now on the cliff top path through a narrow wooded area, which from spring through to late summer offers beautiful displays of many different species of wildflowers.

*A distant view of Lydney Park*

The path winds its way along the cliff top, with views between the trees up river towards Newnham and across to Sharpness Docks on the opposite bank. Ignore the first waymark you come across (this can be a short cut if you wish), and continue to the second one which is immediately before a house with dormered windows (B). Turn left here, walk across the grassed area, and then turn left onto the road. From this point to the end of the walk, there might be the occasional car, so keep an eye out. Enjoy the land side views from this road, including a view of Lydney Park estate in the distance nestled amongst the hills.

At the T-junction (C), turn left onto Naas Lane, going past Naas Court Farm on your right and the overgrown remains of WWII barracks and buildings on your left. Go through the road barrier, and simply continue on this rather rough road until you are back at your starting point. On the way you pass the new golf club on your right, the wonderful and eclectic Naas House on the left, with an old barn opposite, and then, further down, the remains of the old harbour buildings.